Teaching with Multiple Intelligences

Julia Jasmine, M.A.

Teacher Created Materials, Inc.

Cover Design by Darlene Spivak

Made in U.S.A.

ISBN 1-55734-882-0

Order Number TCM 882

Table of Contents

Introduction

The theory of multiple intelligences is one of the most important and promising developments in education today. It is based on the work of Howard Gardner, a developmental psychologist, who set out to create a new theory of cognition as part of his work at Harvard University. Dr. Gardner's original book about the theory, *Frames of Mind* (1983), defined seven basic intelligences that he feels are as fundamental as those traditionally tested for in standard IQ tests. His work was directed toward psychologists but, to his surprise, was embraced by educators and others who are concerned about the quality of our schools.

Indeed, many educators have jumped on Gardner's bandwagon, and the theory is being implemented in a variety of ways from Hawaii to New England and a myriad of points in between. Curriculum is being rewritten, and teachers are being indoctrinated and trained.

This book will attempt to provide a look at the theory—what it is and how it differs from other definitions of so-called learning styles—and at the implementations—which ones seem to be truly valuable and which are merely trendy.

What Is the Theory of Multiple Intelligences?

The Ultimate Validation of Individual Differences

The theory of multiple intelligences is the ultimate validation of the idea that individual differences are important. Its use in education depends on the recognition of, and respect for, each learner's way, or ways, of learning, as well as each learner's special interests and talents. It not only acknowledges these individual differences for practical purposes, such as teaching and assessment, but also accepts them as normal, okay, and even interesting and valuable.

Howard Gardner, whose name is synonymous with this theory, indicates that there could be many more intelligences than the seven he has defined, especially in other cultures. As it stands, the list can be rearranged and subdivided. The real purpose of making a list at all is "to make the case for the plurality of intellect" (Gardner, 1993). Whether or not there could be more, the seven intelligences he has given us are a giant step forward into a place where the individual is respected and diversity is cultivated.

> The theory of multiple intelligences is the ultimate validation of the idea that individual differences are important.

1

The Seven Intelligences

The seven intelligences identified by Gardner (1983) are:

- ◆ Linguistic intelligence
- ◆ Logical-mathematical intelligence
- ◆ Spatial intelligence
- ◆ Musical intelligence
- ◆ Bodily-kinesthetic intelligence
- ◆ Interpersonal intelligence
- ◆ Intrapersonal intelligence

The two intelligences that are listed first are those most commonly recognized and appreciated in our society. They are the ones that assure success on IQ tests and SAT's because they are the ones those tests were designed to test for in the first place. Students who possess and develop the linguistic and logical-mathematical intelligences are virtually assured of success in the traditional school setting. This success is, however, not a good predictor of success in real life (Gardner, 1993).

Students who possess and develop the linguistic and logical-mathematical intelligences are virtually assured of success in the traditional school setting.

Linguistic Intelligence

Linguistic intelligence, which is referred to by some educators and writers as verbal intelligence, is different from the other intelligences because everyone who speaks can be said to possess it at some level. The criteria for more than this basic competence has yet to be set, although it is clear that some people are more linguistically talented than others (Kirschenbaum, 1990). Linguistic intelligence expresses itself in words, both written and oral. People who have this kind of intelligence also have highly developed auditory skills, and they learn by listening. They like to read and write and speak, and they like to play with words. They like words not only for their denotations and connotations but also for their shapes and sounds and for the images they evoke when they are put together in different and unusual ways. Gardner mentions the poet as the exemplar of this kind of intelligence, but it is also found in the crossword puzzle fan or Scrabble addict, as well as in the people on both sides of an acrimonious political debate and in those who make up puns or tell jokes that are plays on words.

People with linguistic intelligence can thrive in the stereotypical academic atmosphere that depends on listening to lectures, taking notes, and being assessed with traditional tests. They are also seen as possessing high levels of the other intelligences because our assessment tools usually rely on verbal responses, no matter which type of intelligence is being assessed (Kirschenbaum, 1990).

Logical-Mathematical Intelligence

Logical-mathematical intelligence includes scientific ability. It is the kind of intelligence studied and documented by Piaget, the kind often characterized as critical thinking and used as part of the scientific method. People with this kind of intelligence like to do things with data: collect and organize, analyze and interpret, conclude and predict. They see patterns and relationships. They like to solve mathematical problems and play strategy games such as checkers and chess. They tend to use graphic organizers both to please themselves and to present their information to others.

Logical-mathematical intelligence has often been revered above other types of intelligence, especially in our technological society. It could be characterized as a left-brain activity.

Spatial Intelligence

Spatial intelligence, which is sometimes called visual or visual/spatial intelligence, is the ability to form and manipulate a mental model (Gardner, 1993). People with this kind of intelligence tend to think in pictures and learn most readily from visual presentations such as movies, pictures, videos, and demonstrations using models and props. They like to draw, paint, or sculpt their ideas and often represent moods and feelings through art. They are good at reading maps and diagrams and they enjoy solving mazes and putting together jigsaw puzzles.

Spatial intelligence is often experienced and expressed through daydreaming, imagining, and pretending (Lazear, 1994). It could be characterized as a right-brain activity and has some characteristics in common with intrapersonal intelligence.

Musical Intelligence

Musical intelligence is referred to by some as rhythmic or musical/rhythmic intelligence. People with this kind of intelligence are sensitive to sounds, environmental as well as musical. They often sing, whistle, or hum while engaging in other activities. They love to listen to music, they may collect CDs and tapes, and they often play an instrument. They sing on key and can remember and vocally reproduce melodies. They may move rhythmically in time to music (or in time to an activity) or make up rhythms and songs to help them remember facts and other information.

Musical intelligence is probably the least understood and, at least in the academic setting, the least encouraged of all the intelligences. Children who hum, whistle, and sing in school are often seen as acting inappropriately or disturbing the class. Many stu-

> **Logical-mathematical intelligence has often been revered above other types of intelligence, especially in our technological society.**

3

dents who are labeled behavior problems are probably out-picturing, or acting out, their musical intelligence. Gauge your own reaction by considering your spontaneous response to a student using earphones to listen to music while reading or doing math.

Bodily-Kinesthetic Intelligence

Bodily-kinesthetic intelligence is sometimes referred to as simply kinesthetic intelligence. People with this kind of intelligence process information through the sensations they feel in their bodies. They like to move around, act things out, and touch the people they are talking to. They are good at both small and large muscle skills and enjoy physical activities and sports of all kinds. They prefer to communicate information by demonstration or modeling. They can express emotion and mood through dance.

Bodily-kinesthetic intelligence is easier to understand than musical intelligence because we all experience it to at least some degree. It is the well-known feeling people have when they get on a bike after many years—the body simply remembers how to ride.

Interpersonal Intelligence

Interpersonal intelligence is out-pictured in the enjoyment of friends and social activities of all kinds and in a reluctance to be alone. People with this kind of intelligence enjoy working in groups, learn while interacting and cooperating, and often serve as mediators of disputes both in a school situation and at home. Cooperative learning methods could have been designed just for them, and probably the designers of cooperative learning activities as an instructional method have this kind of intelligence also.

The dark side of interpersonal intelligence is manipulation; the bright side is empathy. This is the intelligence of the extrovert.

Intrapersonal Intelligence

Intrapersonal intelligence is reflected in a deep awareness of inner feelings. This is the intelligence that allows people to understand themselves, their abilities, and their options. People with intrapersonal intelligence are independent and self-directed with strong opinions on controversial subjects. They have a great sense of self-confidence and enjoy working on their own projects and just being alone.

Intrapersonal intelligence is often associated with intuitive ability. This is the intelligence of the introvert.

People with intrapersonal intelligence are independent and self-directed with strong opinions on controversial subjects.

Intelligence Clusters

No one who is normal has just one type of intelligence, although this unusual situation is recognized and documented in psychological literature in studies of idiot savants or of people who have suffered injuries that have destroyed part of their brains. Indeed, almost everyone has several types of intelligence; some people have them all, although some are more highly developed than others. Even interpersonal and intrapersonal intelligences can occur in the same person who learns to switch back and forth as necessity demands or the opportunity presents itself. Think of the teacher who deals happily and ably with many publics—administrators, colleagues, students, parents, and the community in general—day in and day out but retreats to solitude when on vacation.

There is no evidence that intelligences come in particular patterns or that some tend to be associated with others (Kirschenbaum, 1990). They come in all combinations, and it is quite easy to imagine hypothetical clusters of the seven intelligences. The person with high levels of visual and kinesthetic intelligences may become an artist. Add interpersonal intelligence to that mix and an actor may emerge. The person who combines the linguistic and musical intelligences may write songs or, with the addition of kinesthetic intelligence, perform his or her own music or act in musical theater. The person who combines kinesthetic and intrapersonal intelligences may turn to a sport that stresses individual excellence, such as diving or skating. A cluster of linguistic, mathematical, and intrapersonal intelligences might be represented by the research scientist—reasoning, recording data, and satisfied to be alone in the lab.

The person with high levels of visual and kinesthetic intelligences may become an artist.

It is harder, though, to recognize one's own cluster of intelligences and harder still to recognize those that may be different from one's own in others—students, or anyone else for that matter.

An Unexpected Bonus

Just knowing about the types of intelligences that are a potential for the students one teaches (or the children one labors to raise) can have a major impact on the lives of everyone concerned (students, children, and concerned adults).

On the one hand, if you are responsible for a child who is not responding in the conventional academic areas, you can, with your knowledge of what might be called the "alternative" areas of intelligence, open a new world for that child by exploring his or her responses to less structured learning.

Think of Thomas Edison's mother trying to cope with the genius who had been sent home from school as unteachable. Using the perfect vision afforded to us by hindsight, and knowing that Edison would spend his life inventing marvelous things through a process of unbelievably patient trial and error, we could tell her that he would probably excel if given a chance to use his bodily-kinesthetic intelligence. She simply knew he was not stupid and gave him space to be himself. How much easier for her if she had had some support other than a mother's intuition.

Both Winston Churchill and Albert Einstein were thought incapable of the structured learning of their academic environments. Churchill perfected his mastery of the English language when he was thought to be incapable of learning Latin and Greek. Einstein was just an ordinary mathematics student in his early years. Conversely, if you are responsible for a student who excels in the areas of either linguistic or logical-mathematical intelligence, you can make sure that he or she knows that other areas of learning and appreciation exist. Our colleges and universities acknowledge the benefits of this approach by periodically reinstituting a so-called "breadth" requirement so their graduates will not go through life wearing intellectual blinders.

Becoming Aware of Multiple Intelligences

What We Are Born With

In theory, we are all born with each of the seven basic intelligences, at least to some degree. The more we have of a given intelligence, the easier it will be to become successful in that area. Strong motivation and excellent instruction can help us to increase the functioning of our weaker areas of intelligence, but these areas will probably never be as strong as the areas that started out at higher levels (Sylwester, 1995). Conversely, strong intelligences do not seem to be affected much by formal instruction. A decision has to be made about which is more important: time spent on developing an individual's strengths or time spent on remediating his or her weaknesses.

Cognitive scientists are suggesting that the brains we are born with combine with the experiences we have in childhood to produce the basic functional level (Sylwester, 1995) of each of the intelligences. These levels can be further extended—deliberately or by happenstance—through the experiences we have after childhood.

In theory, we are all born with each of the seven basic intelligences, at least to some degree.

7

How We See Ourselves

Our knowledge of our own intelligences is influenced not only by the comfortable habit patterns that we have built up over the years but also by the intelligences themselves. Logical people look at themselves analytically; linguistic people define themselves with words; bodily-kinesthetic people feel reality "in their bones"; and so on. Unfortunately, we tend to look at others through this same construct of comfortable habit patterns and inherent intelligences. The intelligences we see are "our" intelligences. The world we see is "our" world, and the way we see it is the "right" way.

Without particularly meaning to, and certainly without any ill intent, we then impose this view on other people. As teachers, we impose this view on students, unless we deliberately take the responsibility of looking beyond our own comfort zones.

The world we see is "our" world, and the way we see it is the "right" way.

Seeing Beyond the Comfort Zone

Although the theory of multiple intelligences, or MI as it has come to be known, is very different from old ideas about learning styles and modalities (remember the auditory, visual, and kinesthetic learners—tell me, show me, and let ee do it?), there are some similarities. In the same way that teachers were able to learn how to use that information to see beyond their own styles and modalities, they will also be able to learn to see beyond their own comfortable, natural intelligences. The idea that people are truly different, and that difference is acceptable and valuable, requires a widening of focus, a mental twist, an ability to allow for what one may not easily or automatically see.

It is equally as important for teachers to recognize and understand their own dominant intelligences and learning style(s) as it is for them to acknowledge and accept the learning styles and intelligences of their students. The intelligences brought to the classroom by teachers will obviously impact—for better or for worse—the students who come there to learn because they will affect all of the ways the intelligences can be taught: the environment that is created, the curriculum that is developed, the methodology that is used, and the tools that are employed in the assessment of the students' degrees of success.

Color Blind in a Technicolor World

People who do not see color learn to compensate for their difference in ability by reading the gradations in the different shades of gray that they do see. Nevertheless, because of this difference, their lives are not impacted by color in the same way as are the lives of people who do see color. Scientists who study the ways in which the brain perceives and relays information now tell us that even people who see colors do not necessarily see the same colors (My red is not your red).

The process of recognizing intelligences has some of the same elements as the process used to distinguish colors by those who are color blind. Everyone must find a way to learn to distinguish and even to use those intelligences that do not come naturally to him or her, accepting the fact that the impact of these unfamiliar intelligences may never be as great as it is for people to whom they come naturally, to whom they feel comfortable.

Right-Brained in a Left-Brained World

People who are creative have often been termed right-brained. Although this terminology is no longer taken as seriously as it once was when everyone was rushing off to take a class or workshop in creativity, it is a handy, shorthand way of describing people who do not take logical, sequential, discrete steps in their thinking processes. Left-brained people, on the other hand, those who have been characterized as using traditional critical thinking skills, have sometimes tended to look down on the intuitive thinker or, conversely, sometimes envied and tried to emulate his or her mental freedom.

> **The process of recognizing intelligences has some of the same elements as the process used to distinguish colors by those who are color blind.**

In years past, there was a certain undercurrent of gender correlation associated with these two kinds of thinkers—the serious, logical thinker often being thought of as male and the emotional, creative thinker being thought of as female. Now, however, the ability of both sexes to be "whole-brain" thinkers is recognized and the intuitive leap is no longer termed "woman's intuition." Scientists talk and write about their "ah-ha moments" when everything came together for them and how they went back and checked to verify the steps that their minds must have taken and, much to their surprise, not finding the logical sequence they expected to see.

There are methods for increasing creative ability in the logical among us, as well as ways for the creative to organize and systematize their mental processes (Wonder & Donovan, 1985). The process of identifying and nurturing our intelligences shares some of the same characteristics as the process used in turning right and left-brain thinkers into "whole-brain" or integrated thinkers. It starts with awareness and depends on practice.

Enlarging One's Focus

Learning to recognize multiple intelligences—our own and those of others—is at least partly a matter of enlarging our mental focus. We try so hard to stay focused on the matter at hand, to concentrate, to shut out all distractions, that widening our view of the world can be hard to do. Just recognizing the possibility that there is more out there than your senses are picking up can help.

Have you ever had the rather unsettling experience of learning a new word and then coming across it frequently during the next few days in both your reading and listening experiences? Where was that word before you learned it? Did everyone learn it and begin to use it at the same time you did? More than likely, it was always around. You did not notice it because it was not part of your vocabulary—active or passive, speaking or reading. You "bleeped" right over it as if it did not exist until you consciously made it a part of your repertoire of words.

> **Learning to enlarge one's focus is a matter of changing the lens on one's experiential camera from a zoom lens that takes a detailed closeup to a wide-angle lens that stretches the horizon.**

Have you ever gone to a conference and been invited to take part in this kind of keynote-speech icebreaker? The speaker asks you to spend a few minutes looking around the room (banquet hall, auditorium) and taking note of everything you see that is red. Then you are asked to close your eyes and mentally review what you saw and then open them and re-check the red things in the room to make sure you did not miss anything. "Now," says the speaker, "turn to the person sitting next to you and tell him or her five things you saw that were green."

Most people, if they were caught unaware by this exercise, cannot remember seeing anything at all that was green. They had focused completely on red—observed carefully, visualized, re-checked their observations—to the point where every other color was shut out. The ability to focus in this way is a useful skill if you are able to use it only when you want to and to turn it off, so to speak, when you do not need it. As a standard habit of mind, it can narrow one's perceptions to a degree that much of life, much of the world around one, is shut out.

Learning to enlarge one's focus is a matter of changing the lens on one's experiential camera from a zoom lens that takes a detailed closeup to a wide-angle lens that stretches the horizon. One person may never be able to fully experience all of the intelligences, but it is possible to acknowledge their existence and to perceive their qualities, at least vicariously.

Awareness Exercises

There are various exercises that can help in this endeavor. A very simple one can be done alone, with a partner, or in a group. Each person draws a circle on a piece of paper and divides it into segments that reflect the relative importance of his or her own intelligences. If this is done as an individual activity, it allows people to reflect on the possibility that they may have unexplored areas of intelligence or that there are intelligences that they simply do not experience. (This is your first clue: if you prefer the individual approach to this exercise, you have intrapersonal intelligence.)

If this is done as a partner or group activity, people may get feedback that opens their eyes to talents they have never personally acknowledged, or they may realize that one or more of the intelligences they see in themselves are not apparent to others. (Here is your second clue: this exercise option is comfortable for people with interpersonal intelligence.)

A variation of this activity is simply to prioritize a list of the seven intelligences with "1" being most personally important or most developed and "7" being least important or unrecognized. (People can work alone to prioritize their own intelligences or with partners or groups to exchange perceptions with others.)

A more complex activity is detailed in an article titled "Using Learning Modalities to Celebrate Intelligence" (Samples, 1992). In this article, Bob Samples describes a teachers' workshop in which the participants were asked to "paint a portrait of cooperation." They could use any media they wanted as long as they did not include words, letters, numbers, or conventional symbols. He describes the initial paralysis, the requests for explanations, the eventual explorations, and the final animated discussion of the results. The people involved in this experience went on to design curriculum through which they could share their new knowledge, their new way of seeing the world.

More Awareness Exercises

Educators may also find benefit in variations of some more or less well-known exercises that are often offered as classroom activities. Most of the basic exercises are easy for those with linguistic intelligence and are often just an accepted part of the curriculum. "Write a descriptive paragraph about this picture of a sunset," or "Write a poem about the ocean," sounds like a conventional classroom assignment, but either one will constitute a real stretch for students whose strengths lie mainly in the spatial, musical, or bodily-kinesthetic areas.

On the other hand, "Read this description of a sunset (or of the ocean) and paint a picture of it" will be much harder for the per-

Most of the basic exercises are easy for those with linguistic intelligence and are often just an accepted part of the curriculum.

son whose main strength lies in the linguistic area, and "Read this description of a sunset (or of the ocean) and create a musical composition that interprets it" would probably seem almost impossible to anyone without musical intelligence. Depending on one's level of mathematical expertise, "Write a mathematical description of this picture" might be fun for the logical-mathematical mind and "Describe this musical composition in mathematical terms" could constitute a challenge while seeming like sheer torture to people with most of the other intelligences.

As a workable compromise, an exercise that could help increase awareness without being totally intimidating might consist of listening to a musical selection and using markers or crayons to create a visual interpretation of the sounds. Another activity could be interpreting the music through dance or other informal movement. Less conventional but still possible, might be interpreting a picture, written description, or mathematical equation with movement. Whatever activities constitute a stretch of the intelligences will raise the awareness of the participants.

Teaching the Intelligences

Can the Intelligences Be "Taught"?

So how exactly does one share this new knowledge, this new way of seeing the world? You can explain the theory to people, of course. You can explain it to students as well as to adults. You can list the intelligences, define them, and describe them. You can show students how to think about the intelligences. Meta-intelligence (Lazear, 1994), like metacognition, gives people power. You can consider the effect of learning styles. But can you actually teach the intelligences in the sense of helping someone to attain a particular one?

You can show students how to think about the intelligences.

Reorganize the System

Gardner writes about the process of teaching the intelligences as needing to begin with a reorganization of the school system (Gardner, 1993). He sees the ideal school as a place where individual students will have their intelligences recognized and where they will be placed in a position to use those intelligences, and where their achievements will be evaluated in the context of the same intelligences. He describes a scenario based on a traditional master/apprentice relationship and, he recommends that as part of his reorganization of education.

Gardner sees the growth of intelligence as following a prescribed path or trajectory. The first step in the path is raw intelligence. Different stages in an individual's growth can be recognized through the development of various appropriate symbol systems and then through the specialized notational systems associated with particular intelligences.

Gardner talks about students who are "at promise" and those who are "at risk." Those who are at promise, especially those who are exceptionally talented, often encounter their intelligences through what Gardner calls crystallizing experiences, intense emotional responses that focus the attention and efforts of these individuals in a particular direction. Those who are at risk can be aided by intensive help at the earliest age possible. They may never reach the levels attained by the "at promise" individuals, but they will probably reach a level of competence that is essential in our society; that is, those who are weak in linguistic intelligence can learn to read and write, although they may never become poets. Those who are weak in logical-mathematical intelligence can learn enough computational skills to balance their checkbooks, although they may never become physicists.

Both of these types of individuals can be helped by being placed in an enriched environment. Those at promise will be stimulated by their surroundings to have possible crystallizing experiences. Those "at risk" will be supported in the development of their abilities.

A Memory Model—Explanation

The Memory Model chart on the next page can be used as a script with your class, or as background material for your own explanation of memory. You will probably want to introduce students to only one or two sections at a time.

Although it is a simplistic model and probably does not reflect advanced thinking about the brain, it is a useful mental model. And do not forget that all of the information applies to you, too, and may explain why you keep losing your car keys!

The chart shows in simple form how your memory works. It will give you a mental picture of how you can get things into your memory, make them stay there, and get them out when you want them.

A Memory Model—Chart

MEMORY

	Short Term	Long Term
Kinds	• **Limited** • 7 (+ or -2)	• **Unlimited** • ∞

What gets things in?	What we pay attention to:
	   self
	   emotion
	   different or discrepant
	   mands
		Rehearsal
		Organization
		Elaboration

What keeps things in?	Rehearsal Organization Elaboration	Automatically stays in
What helps retrieve things?	3–8 seconds wait time	Organization Distributed Practice Connectors/Examples (rich/multiple)

Reprinted from Workshop Notebook: How to Organize Your Classroom, *Teacher Created Materials, 1992*

Short-Term and Long-Term Memory

First of all, we speak of both short-term memory and long-term memory. Short-term memory is like a work surface, like the top of your desk. Its capacity is limited. It will hold only a certain number of different items at one time. This number is usually seven, but it varies with different people. Some people can deal with nine different items at a time; some people can deal with only five. (That is what "seven, plus or minus two" means.)

Long-term memory is like a giant file drawer. Its capacity, for all practical purposes, is unlimited. The symbol that looks like an eight on its side is the symbol for infinity; it goes on forever.

Limited Capacity

Let's consider short-term memory first. Since the work surface is limited, things can push each other off the edge. If a student walks into your classroom thinking about the argument with his/her brother, the game he/she is going to play in after school, and the fact that he/she forgot the lunch money, the student will have used up part of his/her short-term memory before getting started on the school day. If the student takes time to talk to a best friend or tries to find his/her math homework before the teacher asks for it, the student will not have space for anything else if he/she is one of those people who can deal with only five items at a time.

What Gets Things In?

So how does anything get in? Look at the second section under short-term memory on the chart on page 15. The things that get in are the things that get your attention. They are very often strong enough to push other items off the edge.

- ◆ Things that have to do with the self get your attention. When the teacher says your name, you pay attention because your name is an important part of you.
- ◆ Things that trigger the emotions get your attention. If something scares you or makes you really happy, it immediately moves into your short-term memory work space no matter what else might be there first.
- ◆ Things that are different or discrepant (out of context, not in the right or usual place) get your attention. If a fire engine came down the street right now with its siren screaming, it would get your attention.

Mands get your attention. This is a fancy psychological term that is the root of words such as "command" and "demand." You stop if someone says, "Halt!" It gets your attention.

These things will get your attention, however, only if they are stronger than what is already in the short-term memory. For example, people who are really sad because a person they love has died will not respond to many of the things that would usually get their attention. That is because what is already in their short-term memory is a strong emotion.

Except in cases of really overpowering emotion, it is also true that you can usually control what is in your short-term memory. You can give yourself a "mand" to clear the work surface and get ready for something new. A student can decide to make up with his/her brother, put the game out of his/her mind until after school, and arrange to borrow lunch money from a friend.

What Keeps Things In?

Since school is all about learning and remembering things, let's say that you have a clear mental work surface, the teacher has gotten your attention, and you are thinking about a concept in social studies. How can you keep this concept in your short-term memory long enough to learn it? In other words, what keeps things in?

Rehearsal keeps things in. If you go over and over something as you would if you were practicing for a part in a play, the things you rehearse will stay in. Another thing that helps is organization. If you have a mental outline with everything grouped under some main headings, you will remember the information much more easily. If you were studying U.S. history and you knew the names of a great many battles, you would have a much better chance of remembering them if you grouped them under mental headings like Revolutionary War, War of 1812, and Civil War, for example. Elaboration also helps to keep things in the short-term memory. Elaboration means making something fancy, adding details to it. If you learn a lot of little facts about one of the battles in the Revolutionary War, you will remember it longer than if you just learn its name.

What Helps Retrieve Things?

Once something is in your short-term memory, how can you retrieve it or get it out? The method that works best for getting something out of your short-term memory, to answer a question for example, is to allow a wait time of three to eight seconds. Your brain needs this time to search for and process things in the same way you might turn over and shuffle through the papers on your desk.

If you have a mental outline with everything grouped under some main headings, you will remember the information much more easily.

Long-Term Processes

The long-term memory is easier to understand and deal with in some ways. The processes that get things into the long-term memory are the same processes that keep things in the short-term memory: rehearsal, organization, and elaboration. And once something is in the long-term memory, it stays there automatically. You do not have to work at it.

The tricky part of long-term memory is getting things out, or retrieving them. Since the storage space is unlimited, there is the possibility of losing something or at least misplacing it.

Organization will help a lot. The more organized you were when you put the information in and the more organized you are about looking for it, the easier it will be to get the information out again. Think about the main headings that you decided on.

Distributed practice will also help you to retrieve something from your long term memory. This is simply practice that takes place every once in a while. If you really learned all those battles when you studied U.S. history, if you rehearsed the information, organized it, and elaborated on it, then it all moved into your long-term memory, and it is still there. If you know you will need to remember the information for a test at the end of the month, practice looking for it in your memory every week or even every few days. Run the information through your mind. When you want it for the test, you will be able to retrieve it easily.

Connectors and examples also help you to retrieve information when you want it. "Rich" means with lots of detail, and "multiple" means many. If you are having trouble retrieving information, think of something that is connected with the subject or think of an example of what you are trying to remember. Your brain may have cross-filed it under another heading. The more details you can think of and the more examples you can come up with, the more chances you have of retrieving the information you want. When you finally come up with what you want, organize it in your mind so that it will be easier to find when you want it again.

Note for Computer Literate Students

Using your memory has many things in common with using a computer. If you are using a word processing program on a computer, you are working in the computer's (short-term) memory. A computer, too, has only a certain amount of memory. When you finish working on a file, you must remember to "save" the information. This is like moving the file from the computer's short-

> Distributed practice will also help you to retrieve something from your long term memory.

term memory into its long-term memory. When you want to deal with the information again—add to it, edit it, or print it—you must load (or retrieve) the file. In order to do this, you must know what you called it. There are times when you cannot remember what you called the file. Then you have to look through the list of files, loading them one at a time, until you find the right one. At that time you may want to become better organized and rename the file so you can find it more easily the next time.

Using Other Mental Models

In the same way that you can use the simple Memory Model Chart with your students, you can use other models to help you use your brain to greater advantage. Current magazines are full of the latest research about the brain and how it learns. These articles are usually accompanied by computer-generated graphics that illustrate the text and make it comprehensible to the lay reader.

The pictures of the brain reconnecting all of its synapses when new information is taken in is particularly fascinating. If you visualize that process, you can practically feel your mental capacity expanding when you learn something new.

Meta-Intelligence

In the same way that thinking about thinking is called metacognition, thinking about the intelligences is often called meta-intelligence. Giving students information about their intelligences gives them ownership of their development. There are many ways of doing this.

In *A Celebration of Neurons*, Robert Sylwester (1995) regroups the seven intelligences into three categories: time and sequence, space and place, and personal and social awareness. The category of time and sequence includes linguistic intelligence, musical intelligence, and logical-mathematical intelligence. We communicate with these intelligences—recalling the past, experiencing the present, and anticipating the future. The category of space and place includes spatial intelligence and bodily-kinesthetic intelligence. We find our way through our environment with these intelligences. The category of personal and social awareness includes the remaining two intelligences: intrapersonal and interpersonal. These two intelligences enable us to look both inward and outward (Sylwester, 1995). A chart of these groupings (on the order of the Memory Model Chart on page 15) would help students to think about the meanings and interrelationships of the intelligences as they develop and use them.

> **Giving students information about their intelligences gives them ownership of their development.**

In *Seven Pathways of Learning*, David Lazear (1994) proposes a metacognitive approach to teaching the intelligences. In essence, it includes recognizing that there are such things as the intelligences, learning how they work and how we measure up, deciding to use them, and consciously using them to the best advantage.

Remember Learning Styles

There are any number of documented learning styles and the studies and diagnostic tools that go with them. Most researchers talk about the styles as if they were permanent features of an individual's approach to learning. Thus, we might have the concrete learner as opposed to the abstract learner, the intrinsically-motivated learner as opposed to the extrinsically-motivated learner, the impulsive learner as opposed to the reflective learner. Gardner feels that styles can vary in the same individual depending upon the intelligence being used. Thus, you might have a learner who is impulsive when using his or her bodily-kinesthetic intelligence and reflective in the use of the linguistic intelligence (Gardner, 1993).

There are any number of documented learning styles and the studies and diagnostic tools that go with them.

Ronald and Serbrenia Sims (1995) include many studies of learning styles in their book, *The Importance of Learning Styles*. In the last chapter they sum up all of the diverse data they have presented as they affect adults. In general, by the time people are adults, each person has developed his or her own method of learning. Each teacher has also developed his or her own teaching style. In order to have the best learning (or teaching) experience, the styles of learner and teacher should be compatible.

This information can be adapted to the education of children by stating it in this way: Children are still developing their learning styles. Teachers have the responsibility of deliberately using as many teaching styles as necessary to be compatible with the learning styles of the children being taught.

Where Shall We Start?

People generally agree, one way or another and depending on the definition of the terms, that the intelligences can be taught. And while we may agree with Gardner's extreme approach and decide that the whole educational structure needs to be torn down and built again from the ground up, we will start with several less dramatic solutions to this problem. We will take a look at some changes that can be made by the teacher in the areas of environment, curriculum, methodology, and assessment.

Environment

Taking the First Step

Once teachers have taken the first step and raised their awareness of their own assortment of intelligences, it is time to take a look at the classroom environment. Teachers are often surprised at how much their classrooms can tell them about their own intelligences. And once this information about classroom environment is noted and evaluated, they are even more surprised at how easy it is to augment, expand, and enrich. Let's take a look around.

Classroom Number One

This classroom is full of books. Some students are working on their portfolios—reading, sorting, writing, reflecting, revising. One bulletin board is devoted to neatly-written samples of student poetry. Three students are sitting quietly, talking about a report they are writing. Two more are playing Scrabble. Another group is whispering while they put the finishing touches on a "Jeopardy" game they intend to challenge the class with. Every five or ten minutes a different student consults a schedule on the bulletin board and goes to conference with the teacher who is sitting at a table in the back of the room.

> **Teachers are often surprised at how much their classrooms can tell them about their own intelligences.**

How can you take this linguistic-dominated classroom and incorporate ideas that encourage the other intelligences?

◆ Put an art center in one corner so students can illustrate their poems, decorate their portfolios, draw, paint, and create with clay. Pull down the maps. Set out a globe. Have tapes for viewing. Make sure the books are well-illustrated. (Spatial)

◆ Add some tape players with earphones and a selection of music for listening. Encourage the groups to talk louder and more often. Allow the use of earplugs (or offer earphones without an audio hookup) to people who want to be quiet. Although most musical instruments will probably disturb too many people, a keyboard with earphones is a real possibility. (Musical)

◆ Watch for people who need to move. Send them on errands. Provide jump ropes, paddle balls, and hula hoops for solitary exercise. Play a tape occasionally and get everyone up and moving. Play a mood tape while students draw their interpretations of the music. Provide lots of manipulatives and things to build with. (Bodily-kinesthetic)

◆ Provide a math center where problem solving can be done. Have it stocked with pencils and graph paper and, depending on the age of your students, counters, manipulatives, rulers, protractors, and compasses. (Logical-mathematical)

◆ Make daily opportunities for group work, discussion, and conversation. Encourage students to plan projects, debate, hold panel discussions, and practice positive oral compliments. (Interpersonal)

◆ Encourage introspective activities such as journaling. Allow students to choose their journaling mediums. Provide colored pencils and markers. Provide tape recorders for students who prefer to create their journaling orally. Make sure that at least part of the journaling is to be kept totally private. (Intrapersonal)

It will be easy to steer at-risk students to the activities that will strengthen their weaker intelligences.

Now, what was a totally linguistic classroom is an environment that will accommodate, stimulate, and help students to discover all of the intelligences. It will be easy to steer at-risk students to the activities that will strengthen their weaker intelligences. At promise students will find enough exciting activities to act as possible catalysts for crystallization experiences in many areas.

Classroom Number Two

This classroom is arranged with the desks on the perimeter and an open space in the middle of the room. The shelves are crowded with beads, blocks, counters, jar lids, scissors, crayons, markers, clay, junk-for-art, science models, and other assorted supplies in general disarray. The room is decorated with three-dimensional student art such as mobiles, string art, and projects in-process.

Some students are working out math problems on the chalkboard. The teacher is with another group acting out a scene from their reading in the open space in the center. The teacher helps by modeling an action.

What does this classroom need? Since this is obviously a bodily-kinesthetic classroom, it needs elements of all the other intelligences, as listed previously, including the things that are found in classroom number one, the linguistic classroom. It will then provide the environment needed by all of the students with all of their various intelligences.

Experiences Outside the Classroom

A child's world must be greater than the one found within the four walls of a classroom, no matter how rich an environment you have created. Some children will, of course, come to school with an enormous background of experiences. Some will come with what might be considered a deficit. Experiences outside the classroom should be planned for "worst case" children. Even though some children who appear in your classroom will already have had most of the experiences you can think of, some experiences will undoubtedly be new to them.

Consider these and add to the list as they occur to you:

◆ Visit museums, zoos, aquariums, and factories.

◆ Attend musical and dramatic performances: symphonies, concerts, operas, musical comedies, plays, anything put on by your local high school drama department.

◆ Go to a local track meet, a gymnastic event, an ice-skating competition, a baseball game, a football game, or a basketball game.

◆ Go to a park and use the equipment: climb, swing, slide, and seesaw.

◆ Arrange a trip to a large amusement park and go on everything.

A child's world must be greater than the one found within the four walls of a classroom, no matter how rich an environment you have created.

- Invite parents and friends to give your students brief music lessons, and then borrow musical instruments and let students experiment with them at their leisure.
- Go roller-blading.
- Go bowling.
- Invite a local high school or college basketball player to give your kids a personal lesson on the playground.
- Organize a trip to a water park.

Watch for signs that one or more of the seven intelligences are being activated in your students. When you are back in the classroom, be ready to suggest follow-up activities that will nurture what has been triggered.

Watch for signs that one or more of the seven intelligences are being activated in your students.

Keeping Track of Outside Experiences

When you organize outside-the-classroom experiences, you will want to be able to connect them to your multiple intelligence curriculum without undue fuss and bother. Many teachers like to prepare for their "regular" field trips by alerting students to what they will be seeing and doing on the trip. Sometimes a student questionnaire is useful for this: Which animal at the zoo was the most interesting? Which picture in the museum was your favorite? Which character in the play did you like best? This same approach, with some modification, can work for the multiple intelligences. A sample of this kind of student questionnaire, modified for use in a multiple intelligences classroom, appears on the next page.

Follow-up Activities

Most teachers also like to provide relevant follow-up activities for their field trips. In the case of outside experiences designed to stimulate the multiple intelligences, you will want to plan ahead to provide the kind of variety you will need. Brainstorming a list of many activities will help you avoid both time-consuming preparation and the feeling of being totally unprepared. A chart that will help you do this follows.

Student Questionnaire for Outside Experiences

Student Name: _____

Experience: _____

You may respond to this questionnaire in writing or by drawing a picture.

1. What did you read, listen to, or talk about? _____

    _____

2. What numbers, graphs, or statistical information did you notice? _____

    _____

    Did you have to figure out anything? _____

3. What did you see? _____

    _____

4. What did you do? _____

    _____

5. What sounds did you hear? _____

    _____

6. Did you discuss anything with other students? _____

    _____

7. Think about your own impressions of this experience. You can make notes or draw pictures/diagrams on the back of this paper if you wish. _____

    _____

    _____

Teacher's Brainstorming Chart for Follow-Up Activities

Jot down activities that will make good follow-up for outside activities:

Intelligences	Activities		
Linguistic			
Logical-Mathematical			
Spatial			
Bodily-Kinesthetic			
Musical			
Interpersonal			
Intrapersonal			

Curriculum

Two Ways to Teach the Intelligences

There are two ways to teach the intelligences through the curriculum: they can be taught "straight," as it were, or infused into the regular curriculum. The culminating activity of the previously mentioned teachers' workshop described by Bob Samples (1992) was an exercise in which the teachers were asked to think of ten to twenty assignments that incorporated approaches that they would not ordinarily associate with the subject matter being taught.

Two different strategies can be used in trying this process. One can begin with the type of intelligence and think of assignments that incorporate various areas of the curriculum. Or, one can take an area of the curriculum and devise an approach that would involve each of the intelligences.

Examples of these two approaches follow on the next two pages. The first example moves from the Interpersonal Intelligence out into the curriculum. The second begins with a curriculum area— in this case, math—and suggests an activity for each of the intelligences.

> There are two ways to teach the intelligences through the curriculum: they can be taught "straight," as it were, or infused into the regular curriculum.

27

Modality Stretches

Curriculum Area: _Social / Interpersonal_

- Make up a "friendship dance" and perform it for a group or for the class.

- Paint a picture of friendship or hatred or love.

- Make up 10 math problems about the people in your class.

- Write a play for your group to perform. Assign roles and direct rehearsals.

- Try to meet one new person a day for a week.

Reprinted from Workshop Notebook: Portfolios and Other Alternative Assessments, *Teacher Created Materials, 1993*

Modality Stretches

Curriculum Area: *Math*

Intrapersonal: Ask children to reflect on and write about their progress in math.

Interpersonal: Start cross-age tutoring with another class.

Linguistic: Ask children to write a story from the point of view of a number.

Logical-Mathematical: Teach kids how to play "Othello" as an exercise in logic.

Visual-Spatial: Create a city / picture using only rectangles, triangles, and circles.

Bodily-Kinesthetic: Stand like a number. Have children approximate numbers with their bodies.

Musical: Find and show a video explaining the relationship of math to music.

Reprinted from Workshop Notebook: Portfolios and Other Alternative Assessments, *Teacher Created Materials,* 1993

Teaching the Intelligences "Straight"

Most teachers do not welcome another area added to their already crowded curriculum. Nevertheless, there are real benefits in teaching by starting from the intelligences and moving out into the curriculum. First and most important, the material involving the intelligences will not be forced, artificial, or insignificant. Second, dealing with the intelligences in an open and above-board manner will automatically involve the processes of meta-intelligence (metacognition applied to the intelligences) with all of its benefits.

The following are some ideas for moving out into the curriculum from a given intelligence. Many more will undoubtedly occur to you on a daily basis as you teach.

Linguistic intelligence can be discussed and then illustrated with activities involving the following:

- ◆ the alphabet
- ◆ phonics
- ◆ spelling
- ◆ reading
- ◆ writing
- ◆ listening
- ◆ talking, discussing, and giving oral reports
- ◆ playing word games and working crossword puzzles

Logical-mathematical intelligence can be discussed and then illustrated with activities involving the following:

- ◆ numbers
- ◆ patterns
- ◆ computation
- ◆ measurement
- ◆ geometry
- ◆ statistics
- ◆ probability
- ◆ problem solving
- ◆ logic
- ◆ games of strategy
- ◆ graphic organizers

Spatial intelligence can be discussed and then illustrated with activities involving the following:

- ◆ movies, videos, pictures, and demonstrations
- ◆ using models and props
- ◆ drawing
- ◆ painting
- ◆ sculpting
- ◆ maps
- ◆ diagrams
- ◆ mazes and jigsaw puzzles
- ◆ imagining and pretending
- ◆ manipulation of mental models

Musical intelligence can be discussed and then illustrated with activities involving the following:

- ◆ listening to music
- ◆ creating music vocally: singing, whistling, humming
- ◆ creating music instrumentally
- ◆ reproducing melodies
- ◆ investigating and responding to sounds, environmental as well as musical
- ◆ participating in rhythmic movement
- ◆ creating rhythms

Bodily-kinesthetic intelligence can be discussed and then illustrated with activities involving the following:

- ◆ large and/or small muscle skills
- ◆ physical activities
- ◆ manipulative materials
- ◆ making and/or building things
- ◆ demonstrations
- ◆ modeling
- ◆ dance
- ◆ sports
- ◆ moving around
- ◆ acting things out
- ◆ body language
- ◆ eye-hand coordination

Musical Intelligence can be discussed and then illustrated with activities involving listening to music.

31

Interpersonal intelligence can be discussed and then illustrated with activities involving the following:

- ◆ cooperative learning groups
- ◆ group projects
- ◆ conflict resolution
- ◆ reaching consensus
- ◆ school and student body responsibility
- ◆ friends and social life
- ◆ empathy

Intrapersonal intelligence can be discussed and then illustrated with activities involving the following:

- ◆ reflection
- ◆ feelings
- ◆ self-analysis
- ◆ self-confidence
- ◆ self-direction
- ◆ self-esteem
- ◆ organization of time
- ◆ planning for the future

However, some of the intelligences are easier to infuse than others and some curricular areas are easier than others to manipulate.

If you decide to use this approach, you will, for at least a part of the day, be coming close to the ideal situation in which students will have direct exposure to the intelligence together with an activity that will reinforce the experience.

Infusing the Intelligences into Curriculum

If you want to keep teaching your regular curriculum without adding another area to your lesson plans, you can endeavor to make sure that all, or as many as possible, of the intelligences are infused into every lesson. Since the infusion should be meaningful, this is not as easy to do as it may appear at first glance. However, some of the intelligences are easier to infuse than others and some curricular areas are easier than others to manipulate.

Most social studies lessons lend themselves nicely to the infusion approach. Using an objective from U.S. history, your lesson plan might look something like this:

Infusion Lesson Plan

Objective: Students will be able to list sequentially and differentiate among the wars in which the U.S. has been involved.

Synopsis of lesson: Over the period of a week (or longer, if necessary) students will review material and...

◆ meet together in cooperative groups to develop strategies for remembering the sequence of the wars in which the U.S. has been involved. (Interpersonal)

◆ design and create a mural showing distinguishing features of the periods in which the wars occurred. (Spatial)

◆ learn a song representative of the period in which a given war occurred. (Musical)

◆ learn a dance representative of the period in which a given war occurred. (Bodily-kinesthetic)

◆ gather data about some aspect of the wars (e.g., countries involved, casualties, length, etc.) and then organize the data in a graph. (Logical-mathematical)

◆ reflect on the values represented by the opposing sides in the conflicts. (Intrapersonal)

◆ write a piece in which you portray the values represented by the opposing sides in one or more of the conflicts; any genre may be used. (Linguistic)

If you were to choose an objective from math or science, this process of infusion would be much more difficult, although there are instances in which it has been done brilliantly.

If you were to choose an objective from math or science, this process of infusion would be much more difficult, although there are instances in which it has been done brilliantly.

In "Multiple Intelligences: Seven Ways to Approach Curriculum," Thomas Armstrong (1994) writes about his experiences in creating a lesson about telling time (logical-mathematical) for first graders. He started by telling an exciting and original story (linguistic) about the O'Clocks, an Irish family with 12 children who lived in the Land of Time. The children—named One, Two, and so on—in this family announced the time hourly with a catchy little rhyme (musical). After hearing the whole story, the first graders took turns standing in front of a huge, handless clock and acting out the role of one of the O'Clock children who, incidentally, each had one tiny hand and one huge hand (bodily-kinesthetic). They went on to play more clock games (interpersonal) with numbers, dance around to the tune of "Rock Around the

Clock" (bodily-kinesthetic/musical), and write stories (linguistic/intrapersonal) illustrated with clock faces (spatial).

This is a curriculum-based lesson that includes (and includes again!) all of the intelligences in a dramatic and playful way. Who would not love to teach this way? But most teachers do not have time to make every one of the infusion lessons they will teach on a day-to-day basis into this kind of a masterpiece. If you are teaching in a self-contained classroom, you will need to infuse the intelligences into your whole curriculum—language arts, mathematics, social studies, science, art, physical education, and music—and you will need to do this every day.

Usually the linguistic intelligence is well covered, and it is easy to check off interpersonal if you use cooperative learning. Most teachers can come up with a logical-mathematical application and invent an art activity for spatial. But what about the others? Fortunately, many of these problems can be solved through the innovative use of educational methodology.

Methodology

Techniques and Strategies

Educational methodology consists of all those techniques and strategies that good teachers have been using for years. While no one can decide if the major efforts of education should go toward supporting students' talents or strengthening their weaknesses, classroom teachers have all along been offering all students as many approaches as possible to learning. Among these multiple approaches are cooperative learning, thematic units, the use of centers, open-ended projects, individualization, emotional context, and the use of technology.

Cooperative Learning

If a teacher is not already using cooperative learning techniques, certainly now is the time to start. Cooperative learning actively engages the interpersonal intelligence, teaches students to work well with others; encourages collaboration, compromise, and consensus; and generally prepares them for the real world of personal and business relationships. The following page presents the four basic components of cooperative learning. Page 37 offers suggestions regarding the teacher's role during cooperative learning activities.

Educational methodology consists of all those techniques and strategies that good teachers have been using for years.

35

Components of Cooperative Learning

There are four basic components of cooperative learning. These components make the difference between cooperative learning and traditional group activities. Many of the group activities you have used in the past can be adapted for cooperative learning by adjusting the activities to include the components listed below.

1. **In cooperative learning, all group members need to work together to accomplish the task.** No one is finished until the whole group is finished. The task or activity needs to be designed so that members are not each completing their own parts but are working to complete one product together.

2. **Cooperative learning groups should be heterogeneous.** It is helpful to start by organizing groups so that there is a balance of abilities within and between groups. You may also wish to consider other variables when balancing groups.

3. **Cooperative learning activities need to be designed so that each student contributes to the group and individual group members can be assessed on their performance.** This can be accomplished by assigning each member a role that is essential to the completion of the task or activity. When input must be gathered from all members of the group, no one can go along for a free ride.

4. **Cooperative learning teams need to know the social as well as the academic objectives of a lesson.** Students need to know what they are expected to learn and how they are supposed to be working together to accomplish the learning. Students need to process or think and talk about how they worked on social skills as well as to evaluate how well their group worked on accomplishing the academic objective. Social skills are not something that students automatically know; these skills need to be taught.

Reprinted from Workshop Notebook: Current Trends: Making Them Work, *Teacher Created Materials, 1991*

The Teacher's Role During Cooperative Lessons

The teacher's role is quite different during cooperative lessons from what it is during a teacher-directed lesson. The teacher has some important decisions to make prior to the lesson, but when the students are working in cooperative groups, the teacher's role is facilitator instead of trainer. When things are running smoothly, the teacher should circulate and observe how the teams are working.

Teachers may need to intervene in the following situations:

1. Get the group back on target if they are unsure of what to do.
2. Give immediate feedback to the group on how they are progressing with the task or activity.
3. Clarify something or give further information to the whole class after observing a general difficulty of mastery.
4. Assist in the development of social skills through praise and group reflection.
5. Encourage or congratulate the group on how they are progressing with the task.

One caution for teachers is to avoid intervening if the group does not need assistance. Part of collaboration is learning how to discuss what comes next, to examine how the group is doing, and to decide when the group is finished. To successfully progress at this, students need time to work through the different stages and to solve their own problems.

Reprinted from Workshop Notebook: Current Trends: Making Them Work, *Teacher Created Materials, 1991*

Thematic Units

For the duration of a thematic unit, most of the activities in a classroom relate to and reinforce the chosen topic. You will find below an organizer for planning activities to meet the intelligences of your students and, on the next two pages, an example of a short thematic unit.

Planning Activities To Meet Learning Styles

Learning Style*	Students with This Style	Unit Activities Utilizing This Style
The linguistic learner likes to play with words in reading, writing, and speaking.		
The logical-mathematical learner likes to experiment with and explore numbers and patterns.		
The spatial learner likes to put his/her visualizations into drawing, building, designing, and creating.		
The musical learner sings, hums, plays instruments, and generally responds and learns to music.		
The kinesthetic learner likes to move, touch, dance, play sports, do crafts, and learn through movement and touch.		
The interpersonal learner shares, compares, cooperates, has lots of friends, and learns with and from others.		
The intrapersonal learner works alone at his/her own pace, producing original, unique work.		

*For more information, see "Different Child, Different Style" *Instructor*, Sept., 1990

Reprinted from Workshop Notebook: Current Trends: Making Them Work, *Teacher Created Materials, 1991*

Theme: Importance of the Sun

Suggested Level: Challenging

Literature: "All Summer in a Day" by Ray Bradbury *The Stories of Ray Bradbury* Knopf, 1980

Poetry: "Sunflakes" by Frank Asch *Sing a Song of Popcorn* selected by Beatrice Schenk de Regniers, et al. Scholastic, 1988

Skills or Concepts:

evolution of the solar system, urban planning, writing about feelings, writing descriptive poetry, simulations of sights and sounds through art and music.

Curriculum Connections:

Language Arts: Science, Social Studies, Math, Art, Music

Summary:

Nine-year-old Margot, born on Earth, remembers the sun, while the children born on Venus do not. They know only the constant rain; however, the sun is slated to shine for one full hour this day, and everyone waits expectantly. Margot yearns for the sun most of all, but a cruel prank from her classmates brings about a tragic conclusion for Margot—and for themselves.

Getting Started:

Brainstorm as a class what the world would be like with constant rain for seven years. How would it look? Feel? Smell? Sound? How would life be different? Dim the lights and play a recording of rain showers and storms. Have the students write in any way they feel comfortable the experience of the rain and lack of sunshine.

Enjoying the Literature:

Read the story aloud, taking care to express the various moods of the story in your vocal intonations. Express the monotony of the constant rain, the excitement of the children, the tension of their conflict with Margot, and their fervor in the sunshine.

Extending the Theme:

Language Arts: Write descriptive poems about the sun, using the couplet written by Margot as a model. Have students describe their feelings when they got something they had really wanted for a long time. Now write about losing something very special that, perhaps, had been taken for granted previously. Discuss the places in the story where the reader can see Margot's reactions to the loss of sun in her life.

Brainstorm what life would be like without rain, plant life, oceans, forests, animals, etc.

Reprinted from Workshop Notebook: Current Trends: Making Them Work, *Teacher Created Materials, 1991*

Theme: Importance of the Sun *(cont.)*

Science: In groups of four or five, plan ways to create a scientific model of the world described in Bradbury's story. As a class, choose the method easiest or best to recreate it, and then do so. This can be as simple or as elaborate as you choose.

Research and study the atmosphere on Venus. Consider especially the possibility and existence of life.

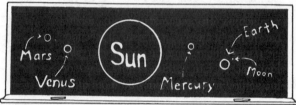

Study the evolutionary history of the solar system.

Social Studies: In small groups, plan and design an underground city. List all special needs (fresh air access, food production, sewage, etc.) and foreseeable problems (transportation, housing, etc.). Suggest a solution for each of these needs and problems in the design of the city.

Brainstorm the reasons why the inhabitants of earth would need or want to move to another planet. Do you think this is likely to happen? How likely is living under the sea or underground?

Math: Create word problems dealing with the sun shining for one hour every seven years. For example, a child is born on February 27, 1990, two days before the sun comes. On May 6, 2004, how many times has that child seen the sun?

Art: Have the students close their eyes and ask them to picture, mentally, what you will read. Reread aloud for them the sequence where the children experience the sun for the first time. Next, provide the students with several mediums (for example, water colors, pastels, crayons, and colored pencils), and tell them to color what they saw in their minds' eyes. Share and display.

Music: Using whatever materials are available in the classroom, have small groups devise ways to recreate the sounds of a rainstorm. With lights dimmed, each group can perform its story for the class.

Related Reading:

"The Fun They Had" by Isaac Asimov from *Earth Is Room Enough* (Doubleday, 1957)

The Martian Chronicles by Ray Bradbury (Doubleday, 1958)

The Green Book by Jill Patton Walsh (Farrar, 1982)

Children's Atlas of Earth Through Time (Rand McNally, 1990)

Reprinted from Workshop Notebook: Current Trends: Making Them Work, *Teacher Created Materials, 1991*

Use of Centers

General suggestions about centers can be found in the chapter titled Environment. A much more structured look at centers that were designed specifically for a multiple intelligences classroom is detailed by Bruce Campbell (1992) in an article that appeared in *Childhood Education*, "Multiple Intelligences In Action." In this article, Campbell tells how he has used centers (as well as an original and innovative combination of thematic units, cooperative groups, and projects) to engage the seven intelligences of his students on a daily basis.

Campbell bases his curriculum on thematic units (see preceding pages). After a main lesson providing an overview of a concept, the student groups spend the greater part of the day rotating through the seven centers. Each student is responsible for completing individual, as well as group assignments. Various approaches are possible at each center, affording all students an opportunity to succeed.

Campbell structures his students' day with time to finish center work, time to keep and share a log, and time to work on individual projects in which the concepts learned in the centers are applied. It takes students about three weeks to complete a project at which time they present the results of their research to the class.

The initial preparation involved in this type of classroom organization is challenging and time consuming (Campbell, 1992). However, according to the author, it soon becomes no more difficult than traditional planning because of several factors: many of the centers are ongoing, activities tend to build on one another, and students take an active part in the planning. If a team of teachers is involved in this kind of teaching, different teachers can prepare centers so the work is divided. Other kinds of centers are also adaptable to the multiple intelligence classroom. They can be very simple such as the Science Center on the next page. Centers can also be very elaborate. On pages 43 through 45, you will find the first pages of a unit describing a center that is stocked with materials and projects that will, with the addition of a requirement for learning a folk dance and song representing different cultures studied throughout the world, involve all of the intelligences.

After a main lesson providing an overview of a concept, the student groups spend the greater part of the day rotating through the seven centers.

A Science Center

Simple as it is, it can meet the needs of all the intelligences, depending on the questions you ask and the challenges you present.

A simple activity center for science can focus on one concept and contain materials that make it possible and interesting for students to explore that concept individually, with a partner, or as a group. The concept of magnetism lends itself to this kind of a center. An appealing standing poster, together with an assortment of magnets and an accumulation of materials to test, perhaps a container of water, and a prepared list of questions to be answered are all that you will need.

(Your materials to test could include metal and plastic paper clips, nails, pencils, erasers, rocks, objects made of glass, candy, small ceramic tiles, pens, marbles, a birthday candle, staples, small toys, steel pins, and brass pins. You should have enough things so the students can generalize from their investigation.)

Reprinted from Workshop Notebook: How to Organize Your Classroom, *Teacher Created Materials, 1992*

Folk Tales from Around the World

A Folk Tale Research Center

Objective

The purpose of this center is to help students develop an awareness of different cultures from around the world through a detailed study of folk tales. Students can do the worksheets individually or work in groups to create their own folk tale research projects.

Preparation

1. Make your research center according to the directions on page 45. Remember that your center can be used year after year, so taking time to make a permanent center by coloring and laminating graphics will pay off later.

2. Assemble a collection of folk tales. Have students bring in their own favorites from home or their public library. Give them homework credit as an incentive. Have them bring in magazines and books showing the cultures of different countries.

3. Reproduce activity pages, and place them in manila envelopes. Attach the envelopes to your center and write appropriate titles.

4. Enlarge a world map. Color and attach it to the middle section of the center. Draw or cut out pictures from magazines of objects from different countries and glue them to your center.

5. Allow six to eight 30–45 minute class periods for students to complete the different activities in this project.

Procedure

1. Have students read folk tales for one or two class periods. Then, introduce the research center and explain the worksheets. For each folk tale they read, have students complete a Folk Tale Research Sheet, and What Is a Folk Tale? In addition, have students write down unique vocabulary words. They should complete a folk tale origin slip and glue or tape it to their world maps. (Options: Have students attach their folk tale origin slips to the large world map on the research center. Or, have groups of students make and color their own large world maps on large sheets of poster board and attach the origin slips.) Use the map to call on students to give one-minute summaries of the folk tales they have read.

Reprinted from Workshop Notebook: How to Organize Your Classroom, *Teacher Created Materials, 1992*

Folk Tales from Around the World *(cont.)*

2. After students have had a chance to read several folk tales have them do a Venn diagram of two stories and graph important characters. Demonstrate the Venn diagram and character graph for your students. Use the example below to show how graphs can be used to compare Nyasha and Manyara. For Nyasha, the X was placed in the upper left corner of the graph because she is both good and smart. The X was placed in the lower right corner of the graph for Manyara because she is bad and foolish.

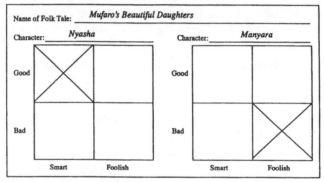

3. Have groups of students make a folk tales big book by organizing their worksheets in a 3-ring binder. Give groups time to discuss book organization, do illustrations for each folk tale, and think of a unique title. Here are some other ideas for groups to research: folk tales from the same country, folk tales about the same topic (wisdom, marriage, origin of something, bravery, etc.), different versions of the same folk tale, comparisons of bad characters, and comparisons of good characters. Make the books available at the research center for other groups to read.

Tips on Managing the Cooperative Group
If you decide to use the research center as a cooperative learning activity, give each member of the group a distinct responsibility. Here are some ideas:

One member keeps the world map up to date by attaching origin slips to the correct country.

One member reports to the whole class about what folk tale topic his/her group is researching. (Be sure to schedule a time each day for these reports.)

One member maintains any supplies the group needs.

One member compiles and organizes the folk tale book that the group presents to the class.

Reprinted from Workshop Notebook: How to Organize Your Classroom, *Teacher Created Materials, 1992*

Folk Tales from Around the World *(cont.)*

Folk Tale Research Center

To make this center you will need:

3 large sheets of poster board

1 sheet posterboard for each group

9" x 12" envelopes to use as holders

collections of folk tales, world atlases, magazines, reference materials

a 3-ring binder for each small group

markers, crayons, colored pencils

masking tape, clear tape

push pins

yarn

scissors

Reprinted from Workshop Notebook: How to Organize Your Classroom, *Teacher Created Materials, 1992*

Open-Ended Projects

The multiple intelligences approach to projects affords a different look at how we want students to learn. Simply put, not everyone will do the same things.

This type of project bears a resemblance to the "jigsaw" method of cooperative learning originated by R. Slavin in which various members of a group are responsible for researching different areas of an assigned topic and bringing their findings back to the group to be taught to the other members and pieced together into a whole (Lyman, Foyle, & Azwell, 1993). In responding to a multiple intelligence project, everyone participates in the same unit or theme but is free to choose the topics and/or the approaches that best suit his or her interests and talents.

Here are suggestions for one way to provide opportunities for students to use their intelligences in an elementary school unit on ecology.

♦ The student with linguistic intelligence can gather information from reference books and literature related to the topic. This student might also want to write a story or report about the topic and make an oral presentation to the class.

♦ The student with logical-mathematical intelligence can collect and organize data about the subject. He or she might want to draw conclusions about the data or write math problems based on real information for the rest of the class to solve.

♦ The student with spatial intelligence will learn best from films, videos, maps, and graphic representations. This student may want to present his or her information in the form of a mural or a series of charts or posters.

♦ The student with bodily-kinesthetic intelligence would probably enjoy doing some experiments. He or she could gather data about the amount of water used each day for one week for bathing and each day for the following week for showering and then compare the results and make some inferences about water use. This student might also enjoy making a miniature rain forest in a terrarium.

♦ The student with musical intelligence could make musical instruments by recycling soft drink bottles (horns), wood blocks (percussion), milk cartons (rattles), and coffee cans (drums) to make an orchestra. This student might also enjoy creating an ecology symphony in which other students could participate.

◆ The student with interpersonal intelligence may want to move out into the community and gather information about local recycling projects. He or she could organize and communicate this information to classmates and their parents to help them know where to take their recyclable materials.

◆ The student with intrapersonal intelligence might want to choose one aspect of ecology and do in-depth research with an emphasis on the values connected with ecological concerns. This student might enjoy spending time in the library, working independently.

Although all of these students will be learning about ecology and probably reporting back to their classmates in one way or another, there is no expectation that anyone will learn or experience all of it. Some students will enjoy taking more than one approach, but it will be possible to succeed by completing just one activity.

It is essential to realize that students do not necessarily know how to select a project, often choosing topics that are either too broad, too narrow, or not suitable for school. Students can be given instruction in how to decide on a project. You may want to actually teach a unit on choosing and completing a project and prepare a list of projects that will address the various intelligences in the context of a given theme or instructional unit. Students also need clear criteria for success in order to set and reach goals (Gardner, 1993).

It is essential to realize that students do not necessarily know how to select a project, often choosing topics that are either too broad or too narrow or not suitable for school.

This method of teaching in a multiple intelligence classroom offers excellent opportunities for increasing students' self-reliance and self-esteem.

Individualization

Gardner's ideal school is an individual-centered school (Gardner, 1993). In lieu of the ideal, anyone can take the ordinary classroom in the ordinary school and individualize the instruction. It involves the old idea of looking at each child to discover where he or she is and then taking that child as far as he or she can go.

This viewpoint is easily applicable to the intelligences because students are at various levels in each intelligence. And though the theory of multiple intelligences tries to turn our society's attention

47

away from its preoccupation with the linguistic and logical-mathematical, even Gardner recognizes and accepts the idea that all children should be offered these areas and helped to reach a level of competency that will make life in our society work for them.

In order to individualize math, for example, it is possible to let the students work in their math books and go as fast as they want to go. They can work alone, in partners, or in groups. They can compete or cooperate. They can check with you when they need to or at pre-selected checkpoints. You, in the meantime, can act as a facilitator and call individuals or gather small groups to work on concepts. In a short time, you will have students working at all different levels where you can remediate deficiencies as they appear and reinforce excellence without neglecting those students who are neither at risk or at promise. As a bonus feature, some students will have a crystallizing experience as they encounter their own "ah-ha" moments and enjoy their own feelings of competence.

In language arts, you can present the students with contracts or let them construct their own. They can increase their skills in the mechanics of reading and writing, or they can read widely (or deeply) and respond to their reading by journaling and in other forms of writing. As in the area of math, you can facilitate the process, strengthening weaknesses and celebrating talents.

This is a method that comes naturally to some teachers and seems risky to others because it tends to greatly empower the students. However, the needs of all the intelligences can be met through individualization.

Emotional Context

Emotion is an important factor in learning because "it drives attention, which drives learning and memory" (Sylwester, 1995, p. 72). Anytime emotion is evoked in a classroom setting, there is a good chance that what is being taught will be remembered.

Good literature can evoke emotion. This is one of the reasons literature-based education has become so popular. Talking about what motivated people in history to do the things they did moves the discussion toward emotions. Activities that involve social interaction provide enjoyment and emotional support. Classroom activities such as dramatizations and role-playing can be laden with emotional overtones that prompt memory. Humor can also elicit positive emotions that make learning memorable. Even emotion-by-accident can reinforce learning. If a fire engine goes

Anytime emotion is evoked in a classroom setting, there is a good chance that what is being taught will be remembered.

screaming by while you are teaching a concept, just the memory of that happening will be apt to trigger the concept, as will the sound of another siren.

Care must be taken not to let emotion slip over into stress. Stress does not reinforce learning whether it is sudden and intense or builds up in small increments over an extended period of time. Many people feel that students and staff alike need to learn techniques that will help them to reduce and control stress.

Altogether, providing a positive emotional context for classroom instruction is an excellent educational method.

Use of Technology

Interacting with a rich environment is one of the key elements leading to intellectual growth. The use of the new technology provides a degree of interactivity that has been heretofore impossible to achieve with traditional learning materials. Educators are also finding that multimedia computer systems have the ability to meet the varying needs of the different intelligences. A huge variety of multimedia applications is available now with new ones coming out every day. Dee Dickinson (1992) in her article "Multiple Technologies for Multiple Intelligences" sorts and lists many of these by intelligence and then offers a list of sources that will be useful to any educator.

The use of the new technology provides a degree of interactivity that has been heretofore impossible to achieve with traditional learning materials.

Multiple Approaches

All of these methods—cooperative learning, thematic units, the use of centers, open-ended projects, individualization, emotional context, and the use of technology—taken singly, in any combination, or all together will help you to teach to the intelligences. You may find that you are already using most or all of them and perhaps calling them by different names.

Short of changing the entire educational system, Gardner himself has not specified any particular way to apply his theory of multiple intelligences to instruction in the classroom. He does not try to exert any kind of control over the schools that are implementing his theories. Consequently, none of the schools applying multiple intelligences is doing the same thing. Some, like the Key School in Indianapolis, Indiana, are giving equal weight to educating each of the seven intelligences. Others, like Hart-Ransom Elementary in Modesto, California, are maintaining a traditional educational system but restructuring the curriculum to give students "at least seven ways to learn it" (Woo, 1995, p. 5).

The bottom line of the MI movement seems to be this: If you learn as much as you can and apply it as well as you know how, your students will benefit in ways that you will probably not be able to document through conventional assessment. While this may sound cynical, there is at least the promise that new ways of "intelligence-fair" assessment are being developed. And in the interim, though things may not get easier for educators, they are getting better for those students whose intelligences are being recognized.

Assessment

Can the Intelligences Be Assessed?

We know for sure that the linguistic and logical-mathematical intelligences can be assessed because we do it all the time. All of the standard tests assess either through language—oral or written—or through mathematical notation combined with language.

IQ tests are language-based; if your intelligence lies elsewhere, you probably will not score high enough to be placed in a gifted program where you might have discovered some of your other intelligences. You may even be labeled below normal and placed in some kind of program where you will be drilled in the basics.

Achievement tests are language-based too; if your intelligence lies elsewhere, you might be placed in a remedial program where, once again, you will be drilled in the basics. If the test was an SAT, you might not get into college. You may never be rewarded for your intelligence because it is not as highly valued by society.

But, can the other intelligences identified by Gardner—spatial, bodily-kinesthetic, musical, interpersonal, and intrapersonal—be assessed? And, if so, how can this be done without filtering the

> We know for sure that the linguistic and logical-mathematical intelligences can be assessed because we do it all the time.

assessment through language, logic, and mathematics? In his account of Project Spectrum, Gardner talks about assessment that will be intelligence-fair. Assessment that is intelligence-fair must be such that an intelligence can be judged directly and not through the medium of another intelligence (Gardner, 1993). Gardner suggests giving students concrete objects to manipulate for all domains. He mentions using bells with which children can play a musical pitch game to assess the musical intelligence and using small figures representing teachers and classmates to assess children's knowledge of social dynamics (interpersonal intelligence).

What Instruments Can Be Used?

What testing instruments and procedures do we have now that will lend themselves to intelligence-fair assessment? Most of the new alternative assessment techniques can be adapted for this purpose. Used in this way, they will, of course, still be subject to the same criticisms they are facing now.

What testing instruments and procedures do we have now that will lend themselves to intelligence-fair assessment?

Critics of alternative assessment methods say they are not reliable. Reliable assessment can be defined as assessment that is consistent, no matter who scores it. This has always been true for normed tests, tests that were tried out on a representative population and standardized to produce percentiles, grade-level equivalencies, and letter grades—all of which could be used for purposes of comparison. The people who believe that reliability, as defined above, is all important seem to be saying that teachers need an outside authority to validate all measurements of progress. They are also saying that all testing must be done objectively, through the linguistic or logical-mathematical intelligences.

Alternative assessment is not objective. In fact, it is subjective. It uses instruments such as observations verified by checklists and anecdotal records and portfolios with rubrics and reflections. It is not exact. Its application may vary from place to place, school to school, teacher to teacher, and student to student. It is a tool for measuring student performance on an ongoing basis.

The types of observation detailed by Gardner in his account of Project Spectrum consist mostly of various kinds of observations which are summarized by the research team at the end of the year. Very young children were involved in this assessment project, so part of the process was designed to identify intelligences. Still, another goal was to make recommendations based on the assessment about steps that should be taken both in school and at home, an area of concern that Gardner feels has been long neglected in favor of norming or ranking.

Application in the Classroom

Although Gardner recommends and does research on intelligence-fair assessment, he looks at the process from the point of view of a psychologist. It is up to educators to take this information and apply it in a way that is consistent with what actually goes on in a school. Teachers are necessarily aware of their accountability both to their administrators and, increasingly, to the parent and taxpayer communities. So, what are the tools that are presently available, and how can teachers use them to assess the seven intelligences and still meet their professional responsibilities? Let's look at the instruments mentioned above—observations verified by checklists and anecdotal records, and portfolios with rubrics and reflections—but, first, a brief glance at diagnosis.

Diagnosis

You may want to get a quick fix on the intelligences represented by the children in your classroom. If you have developed an awareness of your own intelligences and trained yourself to spot different intelligences in others, you will eventually recognize most of the children's talents. But the school year is starting and you want to meet everyone's needs. Besides, there will always be those who mask their intelligences and those who do not know they are talented in a certain area.

This test, also known as the TIMI, makes it easy for the teacher to discover the dominant intelligences of a classroom full of students.

You may want to try a diagnostic test such as the *Teele Inventory of Multiple Intelligences* (Teele, 1994). This test, also known as the TIMI, makes it easy for the teacher to discover the dominant intelligences of a classroom full of students. The results of this test will help you know what you are looking for when you begin to observe. This test also has the added advantage of being independent of language.

Observation

Observation in a classroom sounds easier than it is. Anyone with some experience and empathy can look around a classroom and see what is going on, but in order to be used as an assessment tool, observation must be structured, documented, and repeated at regular intervals.

Observation can be structured by being linked to specific activities. For example, you might decide to formally observe your cooperative groups to determine their level of performance in the area of interpersonal intelligence. After thinking this through, you would design an easy-to-use checklist representing the goals you want your groups to reach.

53

You would then document your observations by using the checklist you designed and repeat this process once a month, once a quarter, or at whatever intervals work for you. This process will give you a consistent record of progress over a period of real time.

Checklists

The checklist mentioned so casually above is not as easy and self-explanatory as it may sound. It is, of course, a list of things to be checked off by the observer. But what things? We have all gotten into the habit of depending on objective, multiple-choice tests designed to measure incremental and, usually, minimum proficiency skills to tell us what our students know. For instance, many reading tests measure knowledge of phonics. A good reader—someone who can read words and comprehend their meaning—who learned to read by generalizing from a sight vocabulary might easily fail a phonics test.

In order to make a meaningful checklist, it is necessary to do a task analysis. Figure out what really goes into the achievement of a particular goal. For example, what characteristics and achievements really represent interpersonal intelligence in a group situation? Put in the things that are important and leave out those that are irrelevant. Try out your checklist a couple of times before you decide to base your whole assessment system on it. Development of a good checklist is worth the time you will need to put into it.

Anecdotal Records

Observation can also be documented through the use of anecdotal records. Anecdotal records used to be lists of comments stated objectively and used to document behavior problems. Now, anecdotal records are positive comments that document the development and growth of students. They depend on teacher interpretation and judgment and focus on the things students can do, not what they cannot do. Anecdotal records can be kept on ordinary paper, but it is convenient to have special forms that will remind you to note the names and dates of your observations.

Portfolios

Portfolios can be thought of as containers in which to gather and store all of the records generated by the new methods of assessment. They can also be thought of as an assessment method which provides a way to take a look at and compare work in order to observe progress over a period of time. Portfolio assessment is most often thought of in connection with written work (thus, documenting the products of the linguistic and logical-mathematical intelligence); however, it is just as possible to collect, store, and

> Portfolios can be thought of as containers in which to gather and store all of the records generated by the new methods of assessment.

compare video and audio tapes documenting products of the spatial, bodily-kinesthetic, musical, and interpersonal intelligences. Art objects; athletic, dance, and musical performances; group activities such as debates—these are all examples that come quickly to mind.

Reflections

Reflections are a form of self-assessment. They engage the intrapersonal intelligence, the hardest intelligence to see in action. Reflections were originally developed for and have been associated with the writing process. They are, however, equally adaptable to any other work that has been completed by a student. They can be removed from the linguistic domain by allowing students to reflect orally using a tape recorder. If students have personal tapes stored in their portfolios, they can rewind, listen to what they previously recorded, and consider the progress they have made before making new comments.

Reflections were once reserved for older students who could express themselves fluently in writing. However, they have been found to work very well with younger students. Younger students may need to approach the reflection process through the use of a specially designed form that will prompt them to think about certain aspects of their work. These students can also work in a one-to-one situation in which they are assisted by an adult or older student who can help them write or record their impressions or listen to their verbal reflections and write down what the students want to say. The very simplest approach to reflection can consist of a series of faces—happy, neutral, and sad—from which the student can select and circle the appropriate one or a blank circle in which the student can draw the face he or she feels is appropriate. Reflections allow the student of any age to begin to take control of his or her own learning process.

> **Reflections allow the student of any age to begin to take control of his or her own learning process.**

Miscellaneous Assessment Tools

Rubrics are a useful addition to the assessment toolbox. The word rubric literally means rule. When used in connection with assessment, a rubric is a scoring guide based on the requirements that were established to differentiate among the degrees of competency displayed in completing a task.

Once upon a time, rubrics were secret documents hidden away and brought out only to grade the writing samples that determined whether a student would pass, fail, or even graduate. Today, however, rubrics are shared with and even developed by students. They are no longer developed just for writing samples but can be constructed for any task. A student who is generating a writing sample or any other product should have free access to the rubric which describes the standards by which the work will be judged.

The last assessment tool might be called translation. It is a technique in which information taken in through one intelligence is put out through another. Students using this technique are often delighted to find that they have knowledge they had never been able to put into words (Samples, 1992).

Summing It Up

We have taken a look at some changes that will help us to teach the intelligences without tearing down the school structure. These ways have included the areas of environment, curriculum, methodology, and assessment. Now, we will take a look at some of the questions people are asking.

Questions People Are Asking

Here, together with brief answers, are some of the most common questions people are asking about the theory of Multiple Intelligences (MI) and related issues.

Who is Howard Gardner?

Dr. Howard Gardner is a developmental psychologist and professor at Harvard University. He has written ten books and has published over 250 articles in scientific journals and magazines. He has won many awards including the 1990 Grawemeyer Award in Education, the 1981 National Psychology Award for Excellence in the Media, and the 1981 MacArthur Prize Fellowship.

Gardner's best-known book is *Frames of Mind: The Theory of Multiple Intelligences* (1983) in which he advanced the theory that all human beings have at least seven different intelligences: linguistic, logical-mathematical, spatial, musical, bodily-kinesthetic, interpersonal, and intrapersonal. Gardner believes that the school system in the United States addresses the linguistic and logical-mathematical intelligences to the exclusion of the others (Johnson, 1994).

> Dr. Howard Gardner is a developmental psychologist and professor at Harvard University.

What is Project Zero?

Project Zero, co-directed by Howard Gardner, is an interdisciplinary, Harvard-based research group that, for the past twenty years, has conducted various studies with teachers and students at different Massachusetts schools. Project Zero has focused on the seven intelligences in the areas of creativity, student projects, and assessment. Gardner has devoted much time and effort to the search for an intelligence-fair method of assessment, but he has found it difficult to separate the assessment from the curriculum (Fernie, 1992).

Has Gardner ever prescribed the ideal way to implement MI in schools?

Gardner has never tried to tell people how to use the theory of multiple intelligences, which is why everyone is doing it differently. He himself has remarked that educators are able to draw diametrically opposed ideas from it. He has, however, made himself available to help and advise as he has done at the Key School in Indianapolis. It is interesting to note that when Gardner was first approached by the people who were later to staff the Key School, he told them that, although he would be glad to help, they were the experts on what went on in schools (Gardner, 1993).

He is adamant that the intelligences should not be used as some new kind of label to limit students' opportunities or ideas about their own options. He also has cautioned that not all seven intelligences can be used to teach everything. Teachers must consider what is sensible and what works (Willis, 1994).

Is Gardner still actively involved with MI?

When Gardner wrote *Frames of Mind*, he addressed it to psychologists and educated lay people. He was very surprised when the theory was widely embraced by educators. He is still associated with the theory of multiple intelligences, at least in the minds of the public and the educators who are struggling to implement his cognitive philosophy.

However, Gardner (1991) has written a new book entitled *The Unschooled Mind: How Children Think and How Schools Should Teach* in which he advances the idea that students come to school with intuitive ideas that are flawed but deeply entrenched. According to Gardner, these ideas are never directly addressed by the educational process and never go away. Gardner's new book doesn't stop with description and analysis; he takes a much more active part in school reform as he goes on to outline his prescription for how to change the schools through a program of projects,

> Gardner has never tried to tell people how to use the theory of multiple intelligences, which is why everyone is doing it differently.

apprenticeships, and association with adult mentors and role models (Gursky, 1992).

What exactly is happening at the Key School?

The Key School has a theme-based curriculum committed to giving equal emphasis to all seven of the multiple intelligences. It was started by a core group of eight teachers as a magnet school in downtown Indianapolis in 1987, and the program has been undergoing continuous modification ever since. Classroom generalists handle most of the instruction, but they have specialists for areas such as art, music, and physical education to increase the quality of education in these areas.

Children gain admission to the school through a lottery and there is very little turnover. Full inclusion is practiced for special needs children who are given special help in the regular classroom. A video portfolio is maintained for each student to document project work, and paper portfolios are being developed. Standardized testing has been de-emphasized, and an assessment system is also being developed based on benchmark work drawn from student portfolios. The video portfolios are presented to the students when they graduate (Mammen, 1993).

> **The Key School has a theme-based curriculum committed to giving equal emphasis to all seven of the multiple intelligences.**

What about the New City School?

The New City School in St. Louis, Missouri began its experiment with multiple intelligences after a visit to the Key School. A committee was formed that began to study Howard Gardner's *Frames of Mind* (1983). From this beginning grew a gradual infusion of the seven intelligences into the curriculum, a variety of modifications in instructional techniques, alternative assessments based on portfolios, and new and improved ways of exchanging information with parents.

The New City School has implemented a much more moderate, even conservative, approach to multiple intelligences than has the Key School. They have maintained their emphasis on standardized testing in addition to the alternative assessments they have developed (Hoerr, 1994).

How do I begin a multiple intelligences program?

According to Patricia Bolanos, the principal of the Key School, in her interview with Lori Mammen of *Think* (1993), the most important requirement is a team of people who share a philosophy, who are willing to work long hours, and—most importantly—who can reach consensus. Everyone involved in a project of this kind must be fully committed to it with no reservations.

How does MI apply to science?

Science adapts well to strategies that include all seven intelligences. After deciding on a topic, teachers can collect activities that apply to each intelligence and allow students to choose a given number from each category. In general, the activities would be of these types:

- ◆ Write a report. (Linguistic)
- ◆ Perform an experiment. (Logical-mathematical)
- ◆ Make a working model. (Spatial)
- ◆ Write a song. (Musical)
- ◆ Organize a dramatic presentation. (Bodily-kinesthetic)
- ◆ Ask three people. (Interpersonal)
- ◆ Decide what you think about... (Intrapersonal)

Teachers find that student interest in science increases greatly when this method is used (Campbell & Burton, 1994).

How does MI apply to the arts?

Gardner says that none of the intelligences is inherently artistic. Each can be used to create artistic works. Elliot Eisner, professor of art and education at Stanford University, feels that the theory of multiple intelligences justifies a much larger role for the arts in the curriculum (Fowler, 1989). Many people say that the spatial, musical, and bodily-kinesthetic intelligences as they express themselves in art, music, and dance are expressions of the human spirit that are necessary for everyone in order to be really well educated. Some people equate the arts with the possibility of a moral renaissance.

How does the theory of MI apply to the gifted?

If research upholds the theory of multiple intelligences, its implications for the education of gifted students are positive ones. A child with talent in one or more of the intelligences could be supported and enriched in those areas of strength without having the frustration of being considered gifted and placed in accelerated classes across the board.

The theory also could lead to a broader identification policy than the one which is based on IQ (linguistic and logical-mathematical) screening. It might then include students whose exceptionally high intelligences lie in other domains (Matthews, 1988).

Gardner says that none of the intelligences is inherently artistic.

How does MI apply to the specially-abled?

Children who are specially-abled can be offered full inclusion in a multiple intelligences classroom. Because there are so many available ways to excel, children who would not be able to succeed in other environments can be admired for their real strengths and talents and, thus, grow in self-reliance and self-esteem.

How does MI apply to early childhood education?

Gardner believes that some intelligences may be time restricted and if not developed early in life may be lost to the individual. Very early stimulation of all seven intelligences can result in higher levels of the intelligences later in life (Johnson, 1994).

How does the theory of multiple intelligences differ from the traditional theories about IQ?

Measurement of IQ is based on only the linguistic and logical-mathematical intelligences. IQ is believed to be fairly stable through life while, according to Gardner, levels of intelligence can change positively through instruction and awareness or negatively through lack of use.

Measurement of IQ is based on only the linguistic and logical-mathematical intelligences.

What is a crystallizing experience?

A crystallizing experience is an individual's overt reaction to an attractive quality of a domain. The individual has a strong affective response that has an effect which can, and usually does, last a lifetime. Gardner cites the effect on Menuhin of hearing a violin for the first time as a child (Gardner, 1993).

Can you use more than one intelligence at a time?

Yes. In fact, according to Gardner, it is almost impossible to use the intelligences in isolation. Actors, for example, would use a cluster of linguistic, bodily-kinesthetic, and interpersonal intelligences. Poets would draw on their intrapersonal and linguistic intelligences. Any of the intelligences can work together. The development of one will not interfere with the development of another, and there are no patterns of the intelligences that are incompatible (Kirschenbaum, 1990).

Will training in one area develop another?

Gardner rejects the ideas of generalization and transference which hold that training in one area carries over to another. He believes in training directly in the area you want to get better in (Johnson, 1994).

What is intelligence-fair assessment?

Intelligence-fair assessment is assessment that deals directly with the results achieved by an intelligence, without filtering the process through the linguistic or logical-mathematical intelligences. Therefore, musical intelligence, for example, would be assessed on performance and spatial intelligence on a product such as a painting, sculpture, or model. Ideally, the assessment of linguistic intelligence would be the only assessment to depend on language (Gardner, 1993).

What is the TIMI?

The TIMI or *Teele Inventory of Multiple Intelligences* is a pictorial inventory consisting of 56 pictures paired in various combinations. Because there is no need to access the linguistic intelligence in using this test, the TIMI supports multicultural, multilingual, and multi-age diversity while directly accessing a student's dominant intelligences (Teele, 1994).

Students should not be categorized according to type of intelligence.

How do stereotypes affect teacher perceptions of the intelligences in students?

Research seems to show that teachers pay more attention to ability and talent than they do to gender, social class, or race if they have information about the accomplishments of students. The implication is that an effort should be made to give teachers as much information as possible about the experiences and talents of their students (Guskin, Peng, & Simon, 1992).

What about the intelligences as the new "labels"?

This is a real danger. Students should not be categorized according to type of intelligence. They also should not be allowed to excuse themselves on the grounds of intelligence: "Oh, I can't do well in sports. I'm a linguistic person."

What are learning modalities?

Learning modalities are the major "ways of knowing" identified by Bruner, Olver, and Greenfield (1967): iconic, enactive, and symbolic.

- ◆ Iconic knowing involves the visual and spatial arts.
- ◆ Enactive knowing involves movement, kinesthetic action, and dance.
- ◆ Symbolic knowing involves reason and logic expressed in coded symbols.

What is tacit knowledge?

Tacit knowledge is knowledge that is not explicitly taught or even verbalized but is necessary for an individual to thrive in a particular environment. Tacit knowledge is a predictor of performance in management. It is a predictor of success in college. It is crucial for success in school.

Although tacit knowledge is knowledge that is not taught, the same knowledge can be taught. At-risk students can sometimes be helped by being taught the information that most people absorb naturally.

Tacit knowledge can be thought of as survival skills. Another name for tacit knowledge is unspoken expectations (Sternberg, Okagaki, & Jackson, 1990).

What questions should I be asking myself when developing my curriculum?

These questions are suggested by Armstrong (1994) in his article "Multiple Intelligences: Seven Ways to Approach Curriculum."

- ◆ How can I use spoken or written language? (Linguistic)
- ◆ How can I include numbers, computation, logic, classification, and critical thinking? (Logical-mathematical)
- ◆ How can I use videos, visualization, visual organizers, color, and art? (Spatial)
- ◆ How can I include musical sounds, environmental sounds, and rhythm? (Musical)
- ◆ How can I include movement, hands-on experience, and eye-hand coordination? (Bodily-kinesthetic)
- ◆ How can I involve students in cooperative groups, peer or cross-age tutoring, and large-group role playing? (Interpersonal)
- ◆ How can I elicit memories, personal feelings, or present options? (Intrapersonal)

Where can I get help in implementing MI in my classroom?

After you have analyzed your own weaknesses and strengths, call on specialists in your own school, district, or community to add their expertise in the areas where you feel you need help. Librarians, art teachers, music teachers, and physical education teachers are all excellent resources.

Check with local universities, colleges, and museums for outreach programs that could supplement your curriculum. Zoos, wild animal parks, and wildlife preserves also often offer instructional and

> At-risk students can sometimes be helped by being taught the information that most people absorb naturally.

experiential activities for children.

Look for MI workshops that are made available through your school district or other agencies.

What is the role of parents in MI?

Parents should be considered resident experts on their children. Receptive teachers can gain knowledge of children's strengths and weaknesses very quickly from parents. Some schools are adopting an official policy of making their first conference of the school year a parent input conference during which time the parents are encouraged to do the talking. Special materials have been developed at some schools to expedite this process. Forms are sent home so parents will know what to expect and can come prepared to share information not only about their child's strengths and weaknesses but also about their child's interests, experiences, and extracurricular activities (Ellison, 1994).

> Receptive teachers can gain knowledge of children's strengths and weaknesses very quickly from parents.

Who are some of the practical experts in the field?

◆ Thomas Armstrong

   Armstrong Creative Training Services, Cloverdale, CA

◆ Patricia Bolanos

   Principal, The Key School, Indianapolis, Indiana

◆ Bruce Campbell

   Cascade Elementary School, Marysville, Washington

◆ Dee Dickinson

   New Horizons for Learning, Seattle

◆ Launa Ellison

   Clara Barton Public School, Minneapolis

◆ Howard Gardner

   Harvard University

◆ Thomas Hoerr

   Director, The New City School, St. Louis, Missouri

◆ Bob Samples

   Hawksong, Boulder, Colorado

◆ Sue Teele

Teele Inventory of Multiple Intelligences (TIMI)
University of California at Riverside

What do the critics say about MI?

Some people disagree with the use of the word intelligences. Al Shanker, head of the American Federation of Teachers, feels that what Gardner calls intelligences are talents (Woo, 1995).

Brown University professor Ted Sizer, founder of the Coalition of Essential Schools, feels that we need the traditional IQ score. He thinks Gardner is ignoring some essential questions about intelligence (Woo, 1995).

Denis Doyle, a senior fellow at Hudson Institute and the founder of Doyle Associates, a change-management consulting firm, feels that developing verbal and mathematical capacity is the major job of the schools and that anything else is a cruel hoax worked on students, especially the disadvantaged (Doyle, 1994).

> Some people disagree with the use of the word intelligences.

Christopher Cross, president of the Council for Basic Education in Washington, D.C., feels that it is entirely proper for schools to put the most emphasis on linguistic and logical mathematical skills since they are the most important ones in our society. He also fears that the intelligences will be used as just one more elaborate tracking system and that no one should be excluded from the common body of knowledge that must be passed along to all students in our schools (Cross, 1994).

Are the critics right?

When one is familiar with the pendulum-like swings of educational philosophy and practice, it becomes easier to step back a little, take a look at the larger picture, and evaluate new ideas in a slightly different way. From one point of view, the critics may indeed be right on one point or another. From another point of view, what difference does it make?

For example, from the position of a practicing educator, what possible difference can it make if one speaks of "linguistic intelligence" or "linguistic talent," "interpersonal intelligence" or "a talent for interpersonal relationships"? This choice of words may be critical for a psychologist but will not really impact the classroom teacher. The classroom teacher will respond to the needs of students, no matter how their abilities are labeled. The important thing is to see beyond the labels and put the ideas into action. Critics who feel that the theory of multiple intelligences will short-change the students whose needs can be identified through traditional IQ testing or bypass the students who most need to develop verbal and mathematical capacity are exaggerating the influence of this theory. Even those schools that have most dramatically reworked their curricula have not thrown out the linguistic and logical-mathematical areas of instruction but merely made room for and highlighted some other, less traditionally emphasized subjects.

The theory of multiple intelligences is a theory that helps educators to identify and empathize with the interests and abilities of all students. It is not a way to narrow education, but rather a method of enlarging, extending, and augmenting the areas of knowledge that schools make available. Although it is not universally accepted, it is a good way to improve the educational arena while all of us search for the perfect answer.

A Practical Application

Into the Classroom

Now that you know more about the theory of multiple intelligences, what will you do about it? If you like what you have learned, if MI rings an intuitive bell with you, if the students in your classroom are already arranging themselves in various arrays of the seven intelligences in your head—here is a plan of action to help you get started using what you have on hand.

Engage the Students' Interest

Get ready to engage the interest of the students in your class by making a large colorful poster advertising the seven intelligences.

Walk into class on Monday morning with this poster and let the students get excited about all the things they will soon be doing. Explain the intelligences using your poster. Give an example of each one. Then, use the lesson plans you made last week and open up the subject for discussion. It could go something like this:

Teacher:

You are going to help me plan today's lessons so that all of the seven intelligences on the poster are involved.

Get ready to engage the interest of the students in your class by making a large colorful poster advertising the seven intelligences.

The first subject in my lesson plan book is reading. I was planning to have you read a story about some of the pioneers who took part in the Westward Movement and then write a story about what you read. That would cover the linguistic intelligence, but what about all the others? What else could we do?

Students:

- We could figure out how far they traveled. (Logical-mathematical)
- We could make a mural on the bulletin board. (Spatial)
- We could build a model of a covered wagon. (Bodily-kinesthetic)
- We could learn one of the songs the pioneers sang. (Musical)
- We could work together to make the mural/model. (Interpersonal)
- We could pretend to be pioneers and keep journals. (Intrapersonal)

or...

Teacher:

The first subject in my lesson plan book is math. I was planning to have you work on solving problems today. That would take care of the logical-mathematical intelligence, but what about all the others? What else could we do?

Students:

- We could work individually (Intrapersonal) to write problems (Linguistic).
- We could work together (Interpersonal) to solve the problems using manipulatives (Bodily-kinesthetic).
- We could illustrate the problems we write (Spatial).
- We could write at least some of our problems about counting the beat in music—like how many half-notes in a bar of sheet music with a given time signature (Musical).

or...

- Have the students set up an assessment process

> That would take care of the logical-mathematical intelligence, but what about all the others?

- Explain to the students what is meant by the term intelligence-fair assessment. Ask them to plan an assessment for each of the activities they suggested.

Reading/Pioneers

- We could figure out how far they traveled. (Logical-mathematical)
- Use a map to demonstrate how the distance traveled was figured. Compare your solution with those of other students.
- We could make a mural on the bulletin board. (Spatial)
- Discuss and appreciate the completed mural. Decide whether or not the details look authentic.
- We could build a model of a covered wagon. (Bodily-kinesthetic)
- Compare the model to pictures of real covered wagons. Explain how it was constructed.
- We could learn one of the songs the pioneers sang. (Musical)
- Perform the song(s) individually or in groups. Entertain other classes that are studying the same time period.
- We could work together to make the mural/model. (Interpersonal)
- Explain and discuss how your group made its decisions. Talk about the different styles represented by the individuals in your group. Did someone assume the role of leader? How?
- We could pretend to be pioneers and keep journals. (Intrapersonal)
- Discuss the experience of keeping a journal. Share its contents if you want to.

Explain to the students what is meant by the term intelligence-fair assessment.

Math/Problem Solving

- We could work individually (Intrapersonal) to write problems. (Linguistic)
- Give the problems to other students to solve.
- We could work together (Interpersonal) to solve the problems using manipulatives. (Bodily-kinesthetic)

♦ Explain and discuss how your group used manipulatives to solve the problems. Did the manipulatives help everyone? Some people?

♦ We could illustrate the problems we write. (Spatial)

♦ Exchange problem papers and look at the drawings. Did any of the drawings help with solving the problems?

♦ We could write at least some of our problems about counting the beat in music—like how many half-notes in a bar of sheet music with a given time signature. (Musical)

♦ Demonstrate counting the musical beat for one or more of the problems. Beat out the time with a partner. Did your rhythms match one another?

Discuss the process of portfolio assessment.

Have Students Make Portfolios

Discuss the process of portfolio assessment. Decide what to keep in the portfolios.

♦ How can students keep records of projects and activities that are not on paper?

♦ Would they like to make video tapes? Audio tapes?

♦ Would they like to take Polaroid pictures?

♦ What standards would they like to establish for their portfolios?

Check on Students' Intelligences

Have students complete a questionnaire like the one on the following page. Repeat the questionnaire at regular intervals. Make your own assessment in the space at the bottom. Use the right side for notes.

Multiple Intelligences

Student's Name _____

Date _____

Write numbers from 1 to 7 to show which of the intelligences is most important to you. (1 = most important and 7 = least important)

_____ Linguistic

_____ Logical-mathematical

_____ Spatial

_____ Bodily-kinesthetic

_____ Musical

_____ Interpersonal

_____ Intrapersonal

Teacher's Record

_____ Linguistic

_____ Logical-mathematical

_____ Spatial

_____ Bodily-kinesthetic

_____ Musical

_____ Interpersonal

_____ Intrapersonal

Have Fun

By this time you and your students should be launched on an "intelligences adventure" that will enrich their educational experience and allow them to take a great deal of the responsibility for what they are learning.

The theory of multiple intelligences is interesting and certainly the most popular trend of the moment in the world of education. It is, however, the application of the theory that will change the way you feel about teaching and students and education in general.

Professional Organizations

National Council of Teachers of English
1111 Kenyon Road
Urbana, IL 61801

International Reading Association
800 Barksdale Road
P.O. Box 8139
Newark, DE 19714-8139

Whole Language Umbrella
c/o WLU
Box 2029
Bloomington, IN 47402-2029

National Science Teachers Association
1742 Connecticut Ave., NW
Washington, D.C. 20009-1171

National Council of Teachers of Mathematics
190 Association Drive
Reston, VA 22091

Association of Supervision and Curriculum Development
1250 N. Pitt Street
Alexandria, VA 22314-1403

National Council for the Social Studies
3501 Newark Street, NW
Washington, D.C. 20016

References

Armstrong, T. (1994). Multiple intelligences: Seven ways to approach curriculum. <u>Educational Leadership, 52</u>(3), 26–28.

Bruner, J., Olver, L., & Greenfield, P. (1967). <u>Studies in cognitive growth</u>. New York: Wiley.

Campbell, B. (1992, Summer). Multiple intelligences in action. <u>Childhood Education, 68</u>(4), 197–201.

Campbell, M., & Burton, V. (1994, April). Learning in their own style. <u>Science and Children, 31</u>(7), 22–24, 39.

Cross, C. (1994, October). Issue. <u>ASCD Update, 36</u>(8), 7.

Dickinson, D. (1992, September). Multiple technologies for multiple intelligences. <u>American School Board Journal, 178</u>(9), A8–A12.

Doyle, D. (1994, October). Issue. <u>ASCD Update, 36</u>(8), 7.

Ellison, L. (1994, October). Issue. <u>ASCD Update, 36</u>(8), 7.

Fernie, D. (1992). Profile: Howard Gardner. <u>Language Arts, 69</u>, 220–227.

Fowler, C. (1989). Recognizing the role of artistic intelligences. <u>Music Educators Journal, 77</u>(1), 24–27.

Gardner, H. (1993). <u>Multiple intelligences: The theory in practice</u>. New York: Basic Books.

Gardner, H. (1991). <u>The unschooled mind: How children think and how schools should teach.</u> New York: Basic Books.

Gardner, H. (1983). <u>Frames of mind: The theory of multiple intelligences</u>. New York: Basic Books.

Gursky, D. (1992). The unschooled mind. <u>Education Digest, 57</u>(8), 27–29.

Guskin, S., Peng, C., & Simon, M. (1992). Do teachers react to "Multiple Intelligences"?: Effects of teachers' stereotypes on judgments and expectancies for students with diverse patterns of giftedness/talent. <u>Gifted Child Quarterly, 36</u>(1), 32–37.

Hoerr, T. (1994). How our school applied multiple intelligences theory. <u>Educational Leadership, 52</u>(3), 67–68.

Johnson, C. (1994, Spring). Howard Gardner: Redefining intelligence. <u>Cardinal Principles, 6</u>(1), 67–69.

Kirschenbaum, R. (1990, November/December). An interview with Howard Gardner. <u>Gifted Child Today, 13</u>(6) 26–32.

Lazear, David. (1994). <u>Seven pathways of learning.</u> Tucson, Arizona: Zephyr Press.

Lyman, L., Foyle, H., & Azwell, T. (1993). <u>Cooperative learning in the elementary classroom.</u> New York: National Education Association.

Mammen, L. (1993, October). Interview with Patricia Bolanos. <u>Think, 4</u>(1), 3–11.

Matthews, D. (1988). Gardner's multiple intelligence theory: An evaluation of relevant research literature and a consideration of its application to gifted education. <u>Roeper Review, 11</u>(2), 32–36.

Samples, Bob. (1992). Using learning modalities to celebrate intelligence. <u>Educational Leadership, 50</u>(2), 62–66.

Sims, R. and Sims, S. (1995). <u>The importance of learning styles.</u> Westport, CT: Greenwood Press.